Safety First!

Safety on the Playground

by Lucia Raatma

Consultants:
Donna J. Thompson, Ph.D., Director
Susan D. Hudson, Ph.D., Project Associate
Mick Mack, Ph.D., Project Coordinator
National Program for Playground Safety
University of Northern Iowa, Cedar Falls, Iowa

Bridgestone Books
an imprint of Capstone Press
Mankato, Minnesota

Bridgestone Books are published by Capstone Press
818 North Willow Street, Mankato, Minnesota 56001
http://www.capstone-press.com

Library of Congress Cataloging-in-Publication Data
Raatma, Lucia.
Safety on the playground/by Lucia Raatma.
    p. cm.—(Safety first)
Includes bibliographical references (p. 24) and index.
Summary: Discusses how to safely use swings, slides, and
other playground equipment.
ISBN 0-7368-0062-X
1. Playgrounds—Safety measures—Juvenile literature.
[1. Playgrounds—Safety measures. 2. Safety.] I. Title. II. Series.
GV424.R22 1999
796'.06'8—dc21   98-18585
                                                                        CIP
                                                                        AC

Editorial Credits

Rebecca Glaser, editor; Clay Schotzko/Icon Productions, cover designer;
  Sheri Gosewisch, photo researcher

Photo Credits

Betty Crowell, 16
David Clobes, cover, 10
James Hazelwood, 6
James L. Shaffer, 4, 12,18
Lattin Photos, 8, 20
Unicorn Stock Photos/Robert W. Ginn, 14

Table of Contents

Safe Playgrounds

Playgrounds are fun places where children play. But children can get hurt if they are not careful. You can learn how to prevent accidents on playgrounds.

What to Wear

You should wear safe clothes when you play. Wear clothes with no strings. Strings could get caught on slides, swings, or other playground equipment. Wear shoes when you play. Tie them tightly so you do not trip.

Playground Surfaces

Playgrounds with soft surfaces under the equipment are safest. Soft surfaces are sand, pea gravel, wood chips, and rubber. Do not use playground equipment that is over a hard surface. Hard surfaces are asphalt, concrete, dirt, and grass.

Broken Equipment

Broken playground equipment is not safe. Watch for any loose parts or open hooks. Hooks on swings should be closed. Tell an adult if you see broken equipment. Do not play on broken equipment until someone fixes it.

Climbing Safely

Climbing equipment should stand over a soft surface. Use both hands when you climb. Climb only on dry equipment. You could fall if it is wet.

Safety on Swings

Sit down while you swing. Slow down before you get off a swing. You could get hurt if you jump. Do not walk near someone who is swinging. You could get hit if you walk too close.

Safety on Slides

Never climb up the front of the slide. Someone may slide down and hit you. Use the ladder instead. Hold on with both hands as you climb. It is safest to slide down feet first. Only one person should slide down at a time.

Safety during Games

Children often play running games on fields at playgrounds. Be sure to stay away from areas with equipment. You could run into slides or swings if you play too close.

Strangers

Play at playgrounds only when an adult you know is watching you. Stay away from strangers. A stranger is anyone you do not know. Stay close to your friends while you play. Never leave the playground with someone you do not know.

Hands on: Egg Drop

You may get hurt if you fall off playground equipment. Soft surfaces keep you from becoming badly hurt. This activity will show you which surfaces are safest.

What You Need
newspaper

shoebox(es)

sand or wood chips

eggs

concrete block

What You Do
1. Cover an area on the floor with newspaper.
2. Fill the shoebox with sand and place it on the newspaper.
3. Hold an egg about three feet (1 meter) above the sand. Drop the egg. What happens?
4. Place the concrete block on the newspaper.
5. Hold one egg about three feet (1 meter) above the concrete block. Drop the egg. What happens?
6. You also can test different surfaces. Fill another shoebox with pea gravel, wood chips, or rubber. Drop an egg on each new surface you try. What happens?
7. You can test different hard surfaces too. Try dropping an egg on grass, asphalt, or dirt. What happens?

The egg should not break on the soft surfaces. The hard surfaces will cause the egg to break. You should always choose playgrounds with soft surfaces under the equipment.

Words to Know

accident (AK-si-duhnt)—when a person is hurt; people do not expect accidents.

asphalt (ASS-fawlt)—a black tar that is mixed with sand and gravel to make paved roads; asphalt is a hard playground surface.

concrete (con-CREET)—a mix that gets hard when it dries; concrete is a hard playground surface.

pea gravel (PEE GRAV-uhl)—small stones the size of peas; pea gravel is a soft playground surface.

playground equipment (PLAY-grownd i-KWIP-muhnt)—things that children play or climb on; slides and swings are playground equipment.

stranger (STRAYN-jur)—anyone you do not know

surface (SUR-fiss)—the top layer of something; sand, pea gravel, wood chips, and rubber are soft playground surfaces.

Read More

Boelts, Maribeth. *A Kid's Guide to Staying Safe at Playgrounds.* The Kid's Library of Personal Safety. New York: PowerKids Press, 1997.
Raatma, Lucia. *Safety around Strangers.* Safety First! Mankato, Minn.: Bridgestone Books, 1999.

Internet Sites

Kids' Safety Tips
http://www.incomecafe.com/kidstips.htm
National Program for Playground Safety
http://www.uni.edu/playground
Stay Alert, Stay Safe
http://www.sass.ca/kmenu.htm

Index